MUSICAL GAMES

FOR CHILDREN OF ALL AGES

By ESTHER L. NELSON

Illustrations by SHIZU MATSUDA

STERLING PUBLISHING CO., INC. NEW YORK

OTHER BOOKS OF INTEREST

Best Singing Games for Children of All Ages
Dancing Games for Children of All Ages
Holiday Singing and Dancing Games
Make Your Own Musical Instruments
Movement Games for Children of All Ages
Playing and Composing on the Recorder
The Rhythm Band Book
The Silly Songbook
Singing and Dancing Games for the Very Young

Sincere thanks to Mara Sokolsky for her help in gathering material for this book and her help in writing it, and to my editor, Sheila Barry, for her good sense and infallible taste.

And further thanks to friends and colleagues for sharing their knowledge with me—Anna Cole, Elsie Falls, Judy Felsenfeld, Doris Green, Lee Hurwitch (U.S. Embassy, Santa Domingo), Carmen Jackson, Shulamit Kornberg Kivel, Mike Lerner, Paula Levine, Stanley Marlin, the New Zealand Embassy, Lael Weissman, Astair Zekiros.

CONTENTS

To my mother, Freda Nelson,
for sharing her love of music with me.

BEFORE YOU BEGIN

Here are lots of different ways to have musical fun. Music doesn't come only from instruments. Use your body, move it to rhythm, clap your hands, your shoulders, your knees, to create your own rhythm orchestra. Use your voice—chant, sing alone or in a group, do it in parts and rounds.

The piano arrangements in this book are as simple as possible. For many of the games you need them just to give you an idea of the tune or rhythm. But any musical accompaniment helps when you're singing and dancing, and you need only a small knowledge of playing to follow these.

If you play the autoharp, the zither, the guitar or banjo, instead of (or in addition to) the piano, use them whenever you can. They make the music even richer.

You can play some of the games alone (such as ball bouncing), some with one partner (like pat-a-cake). Some are especially good for small groups (jumping rope or jigsaw songs). Most of them work wonderfully with larger groups, even if you're planning to include a whole class of up to 30 people. If you don't have enough space for that number, divide the people into two groups and play the game twice. Or have two groups playing at the same time.

This book starts with simple songs that you can move with, play with or just sing for the fun of the silly words. Even the youngest children enjoy them—songs like "Me and My Horse," and "Poor Little Jerry." The bulk of the songs, dances and games are especially popular with 5- to 12-year-olds, but with many of them, the age range is unlimited. Older children and adults love square dances, for example. You'll find suggested age ranges at the back of the book, but don't let them limit you. Feel free to invent your own more difficult versions of the easy games, if you're with an older group. Simplify complex ones for younger players. A few ideas for these variations are spelled out in the instructions, but no game should be rigid. Even if you're doing an "authentic" folk dance, it is only someone's version of it. Change it, re-arrange it—add and subtract. Maybe you'll be going back to an even more authentic lost original!

Make up new lyrics to amuse your group; slip in its own jokes and activities. "Zipper" in names of people in the room. You'll probably improve your co-ordination, develop your musical ear, get thinner, walk taller, move more gracefully. But it will all happen more easily and quickly if you enjoy what you're doing!

Have fun!

I HUG MYSELF 'CAUSE I LOVE ME SO!

Number of players: Unlimited

Gutsy

Oh, I love my knees, and I give them a squeeze, and I bend them and stretch them

as I please. I____ love my toes, and I love my nose, and I

wig-gle, wig-gle, wig-gle them un-til they grows. I lo-ve my back, and I

give it a slap. I cu-rl it up and I give it a nap. I

love my head and I take it to bed, and I shake it hard ti-ll it turns red.

I HUG MYSELF 'CAUSE I LOVE ME SO!

This song is self-explanatory. Sit or stand or lie down as you sing it. Play with it, find new movements to do to it each time. Anything goes!

Oh, I love my knees,
And I give them a squeeze,
And I bend them and stretch them as I please.

I love my toes,
And I love my nose,
And I wiggle, wiggle, wiggle them until they grows.

I love my back,
And I give it a slap,
I curl it up and I give it a nap.

I love my head,
And I take it to bed,
And I shake it hard till it turns red.

Oh, I love my feet,
'Cause they're so neat,
And I kick them high till they fly in the street.

I love my shoulders,
'Cause they can shake
Up and down, up and down and around the lake.

I love my hips,
And I take them on trips,
And I twirl them and swirl them
With lots of dips.

Around and around and around I go
And I hug myself,
'Cause I love me so!

TWO TWIN AIRPLANES

Sing this finger game to the tune of "Frère Jacques." Your hands tell the story as you sing. Make them into airplanes. One way to form a plane with your hand is to keep your 3 middle fingers together as the body of the plane. Stretch your thumb and pinky away from the body to form the wings. Now the plane is ready to take off.

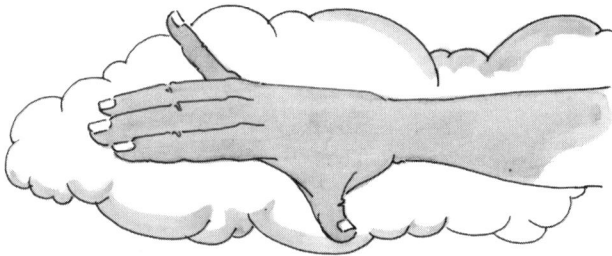

As you sing the first 2 lines, the planes slide along the runway (any flat surface). On line 3 they take off. The planes circle and do tricks in the air until the end of the first stanza.

In the second stanza, one of the planes flutters as it flies. It plunges from the sky into the water. Once on the waves, it rocks gently from side to side.

In the third stanza, slide the other hand under the belly of the plane that has gone down. The fingers of this hand become the passengers. They gradually slip out from under the plane with an undulating motion, swimming ashore. The passengers tremble with "cold and wet." They swim back to the plane on line 6. For the last 2 lines, give the plane a new formation: place one hand flat over the other and keep your fingers together. Extend your thumbs for wings.

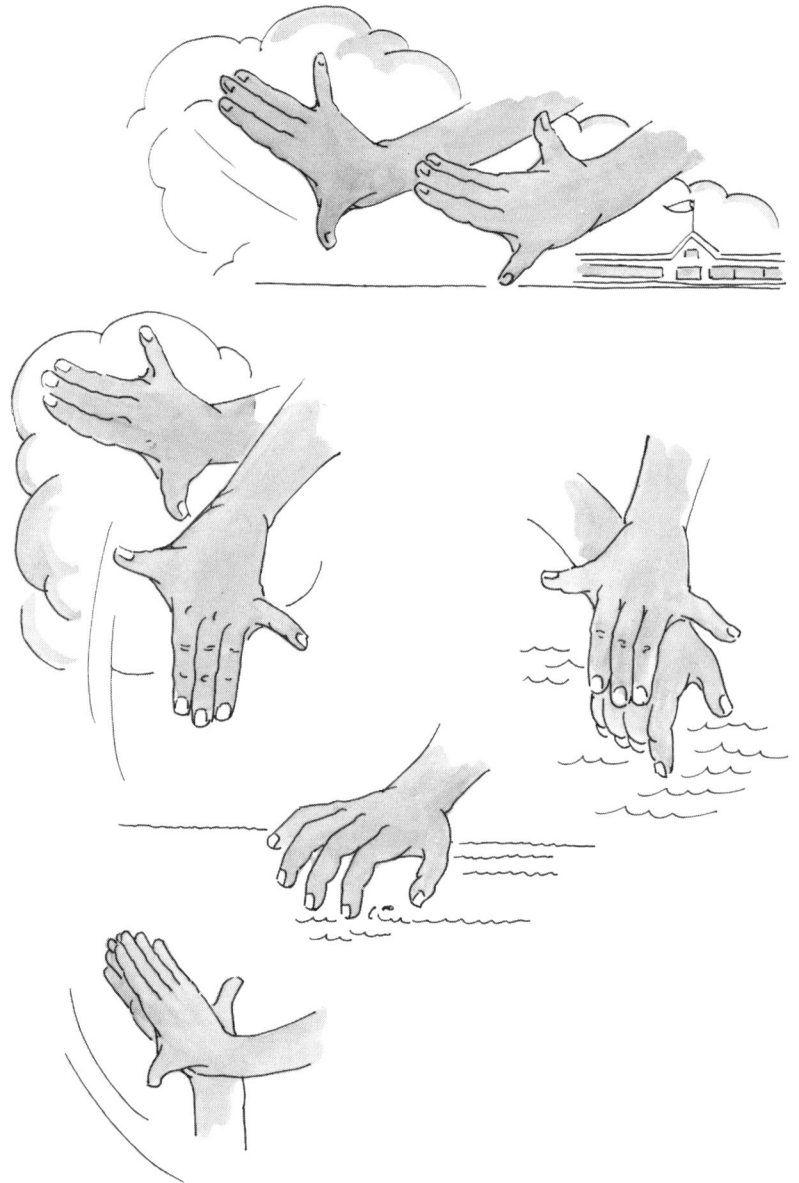

TWO TWIN AIRPLANES

Number of players: Unlimited

Two twin air - planes, Two twin air - planes, Fly - ing

high, Fly - ing high, Cir - cl - ing and turn - ing,

Ty - ing knots and whirl - ing, In the sky, In the sky.

1

Two twin airplanes,
Two twin airplanes,
Flying high,
Flying high,
Circling and turning,
Tying knots and whirling,
In the sky,
In the sky.

2

Two twin airplanes,
Two twin airplanes,
Flying high,
Flying high.
One of them has no gas,
One of them has no gas,
Oh, too bad,
Oh, too bad!

3

Five five passengers,
Five five passengers,
Swim ashore,
Swim ashore,
Hungry, cold and wet,
But I'll make a bet
They'll fly some more—
Fly some more!

POOR LITTLE JERRY

Seriously

All a-lone for a loaf of bread, Went lit-tle Jer-ry.

"Watch the sig-nals," his moth-er said, "Yes," an-swered Jer-ry. But

he for-got what his moth-er said and he for-got when the light turned red. He

felt a big bump and he thought he was dead, Poor lit-tle Jer-ry.

POOR LITTLE JERRY

If you sing this dramatic song with a group, just sit around the piano or on the floor. You might assign parts and act it out, but it is just as much fun with pantomime movements, or none at all.

All alone for a loaf of bread,
Went little Jerry.
"Watch the signals," his mother said,
"Yes," answered Jerry.

But he forgot what his mother said
And he forgot when the light turned red.
He felt a big bump and he thought he was dead,
Poor little Jerry.

They bundled him up and they put him to bed.
Poor little Jerry.
"You're lucky you're living," the doctor said.
"Yes," answered Jerry.

They fixed his arm and they bandaged his head.
"I'll never do that again," he said.
"I'll always stop when the light turns red,"
Smart little Jerry.

GALLINITA CIEGA (Blind Chicken)

Number of players: Unlimited

This version of "Blind Man's Buff" is from Peru. Choose one child to be the Chicken, who is blindfolded and stands in the center of the room. The other children form a circle around him or her. One of them turns Chicken in place as the circle chants:

"Gallinita ciega,   "Blind little chicken,
¿Qué se te had perdido?"   What have you lost?"

Chicken keeps turning independently and answers:

"Una aguja y un dedal."   "A needle and thimble."

The group asks:

"¿Dondé?"   "Where did you lose them?"

Chicken keeps turning, but may stop and reverse direction if he or she chooses, and answers:

"En el gallinero."   "In the chicken coop."

The group replies:
"Pues ponte a buscarlos."   "Well, go look for them."

The same one who started Chicken turning gives Chicken a gentle push and everyone moves away. They hover near Chicken, keeping out of reach but making teasing, clucking sounds. They can stick their tongues out and make faces, too, if they want.

Chicken tries to tag somebody and when a child is caught, he or she becomes the next Chicken. The old Chicken starts the new Chicken turning, and the game repeats.

ME AND MY HORSE

Lilting

Number of players: Unlimited

Me and my horse go hip - pi - ty hop - pi - ty, Me and my horse go

clip - pi - ty clop - pi - ty, As we go rid - ing jig - gi - ty, jog - gi - ty,

o - ver the roll - ing plain.

ME AND MY HORSE

Me and my horse go hippity hoppity,
Me and my horse go clippity cloppity,
As we go riding jiggity joggity,
Over the rolling plain.

It is spring the daisies are popping out.
It is spring the grass is tender,
As we go riding jiggity joggity,
Over the rolling plain.

You can hear the lope and feel the movement of the horse as he gallops along in this song. If you sing it with a large number of people, divide the group into two parts. While one section sings the song, the other makes clicking sounds in a galloping rhythm:

Change parts on the second stanza, so everyone has a turn to make the clicking sound of horses' hooves. You can also make the click with rhythm sticks or any percussive instruments—drums, tambourines—by using your shoes to beat out the rhythm against each other, or even by tapping on the floor with your hands.

When the singers and the orchestra are playing well, you can add horses and riders. Choose partners: the horse stretches arms out in back, and the rider holds onto them, or the rider can hold onto the waist of the horse.

In the first stanza, horses and riders gallop away over the field. In the first line of the second stanza, they slow down almost to a stop, while the rider bends down to pick some daisies. On the second line, the horse bends way down in front to eat the grass (the rider has to be careful not to fall off, when this happens). For the last two lines, away they gallop once more. The horse and rider should change parts so they each get a chance at the other role. And don't forget the orchestra and the singers—they can be horses and riders, too.

ANIMAL FAIR

Number of players: Unlimited

I went to the an-i-mal fair. The birds and the beasts were there. The

old ba-boon by the light of the moon was comb-ing his au-burn hair. The

mon-key he had spunk, and stepped on the el - e-phant's trunk. The el - e -phant sneezed and

fell on his knees, And that was the end of the monk, the monk, the monk, the monk...

14

ANIMAL FAIR

An entire group can sing this vivacious song together, but it is more interesting to break the group into two parts: one sings the melody while the other sings only "The monk, the monk, the monk, the monk . . ." This is actually the harder part; it is difficult to keep going against the melody. When the first group comes to the end of the song and starts singing "the monk" part, it continues with it, while the second group sings the melodic line.

AMPÉ (1-2-3-Shoot–African Style)

This children's game comes from southern Ghana, but it is also played in other African countries. Two girls play it together, or a girl and boy, but two boys never play it together! They play a special Boys' Ampé, which you'll see later.

You've probably played a similar game when you need to pick someone as the leader or decide who goes first. You and your partner each make a fist, choose "Odds" or "Evens," and say, "1–2–3–Shoot," and you each shoot out one or two fingers. If you both put out the same number of fingers, "Evens" gains a point. If you put out different fingers, "Odds" gains a point. Three points wins.

In this African game, you face your partner, clap your hands on "One" and "Two," and on "Three," stick out one foot in front. If you both stick out a foot on the same side (one the left foot and the other the right foot), "Evens" wins the point. If you stick out opposite feet (both right or both left), "Odds" wins. In Ghana, children play the game for the sheer fun of it, not for choosing. The game goes on until one person wins by getting 11 points.

Number of players: Unlimited partners

After a few rounds, the game gets more complex. You jump after the second clap, before you extend your foot. As the game progresses, you do tricks after the jump—clap your feet, cross them over and back, click your heels—whatever you want. When you land, pause for a fourth count, see who has won the point, and start again.

Boys' Ampé

Two boys sit or squat. They clap their hands on their knees for "One" and "Two" and shoot their fingers out on "Three," (as in our version). Sometimes they keep their hands behind their backs. They can shoot out one or two fingers from either hand, and even switch from one hand to the other, if they choose.

Group Ampé:

Form a circle with "It" in the center. "It" walks around and then stops in front of someone, calls "Odds" or "Evens," and the two play the game. If "It" loses, the other person becomes the new "It." And the game goes on.

OH, I HAD A SILLY CHICKEN

Number of players: Unlimited

Oh, I had a sil-ly chick-en and he would-n't lay an egg, So I poured hot wa-ter up and down his leg, And he gig-gled And he gig-gled And he gig-gled all the day, And my poor lit-tle chick-en laid a hard-boiled egg.

This wonderfully spirited song is great for clapping. Start with:

Next time clap it twice as fast, like this:

Now make it twice as fast as the last one, so it looks like this:

This time clap each line in this rhythm:

If you are in a large group, divide it into three parts. Each one claps a different rhythm. Start with one group clapping, and then add groups until all 3 different rhythms are going at the same time. It isn't easy, but it's fun, especially if you sing the words as you do it.

16

PERUVIAN WOLF GAME

Number of players: 8 - 20

Ju - gue - mos en el bos - que, Mien - tras el lo - bo no es - tá. Lo - bo, es - tás?

Choose one child to be the wolf, who curls up in a corner of the room as if asleep. Two of the other corners are "Safe" or "Base." The rest of the children take hands and form a circle in the center of the room. As they walk around the circle, they sing the chorus:

"Juguemos en el bosque,   "Let's play in the forest,
Mientras el lobo no está."   While the wolf is away."

Now the circle stops and the children shout:

"¿Lobo, estás?"   "Wolf, are you there?"

Wolf answers in a deep, ominous voice:

"Estoy levantándome   "I am just getting
de la cama."   out of bed."

Wolf acts out all the answers. Remember that, in pantomime, movements are larger than life. Exaggerate them!

The circle walks again, sings the chorus and shouts "¿Lobo estás?" This time, Wolf might answer:

"Lavándome los dientes."   "I am brushing my teeth."

As the game continues, Wolf is free to make up any number of answers. For example:

"Estoy peinándome la melena."   "I am brushing my hair."

"Estoy afilándome las garras."   "I am sharpening my claws."

"Estoy desayunándome una oveja."   "I am eating a sheep for breakfast."

When Wolf is ready, in reply to the question, "Wolf, are you there?" Wolf shouts:

"¡Aqui estoy!"   "Here I am!"

Wolf rushes at the circle trying to tag someone who will become the next Wolf. Those in the circle run to the two safe corners, and they can stay there for the amount of time it takes to say, "Lobo" 5 times. This keeps constant movement going between the two corners and elsewhere in the room, until Wolf catches someone. The new Wolf goes into the far corner, curls up, and the game starts again.

Play the game 2 or 3 times, but not more than that. The drama is lost with too much repetition.

IF YOU'RE HAPPY AND YOU KNOW IT

Very perky

If you're hap - py and you know it, clap your hands, (clap clap) If you're

hap - py and you know it, clap your hands, (clap clap) If you're hap - py and you know it, Then you

real - ly ought to show it, If you're hap - py and you know it, clap your hands. (clap clap)

IF YOU'RE HAPPY AND YOU KNOW IT

Sing this happy song while you do a circle dance. Join hands in a circle. As you sing the word "happy" in the first line, start tip-toeing quietly to the center of the circle with 5 small steps. Then clap twice.

Repeat the same thing backing out of the circle on the second line, still very quietly.

On the third and fourth line, let loose! Skip around yourself in place 8 times. Shake your hands, your head, your hips—whatever moves—in a free and spirited way —and sing out loudly. Finish your last skip facing the center of the circle.

On the last line, take 3 little jumps in place, leaving space between each one. Then do the last 2 claps really loud and jump high in the air. You may want to try a different form of clapping—once in front of you and once behind you—over your head, under your legs, on the floor.

When you repeat the dance, change the lyrics of the song. Instead of "Clap your hands," try these variations:

> **stamp your feet (stamp stamp)**
> **snap your fingers (snap snap)**
> **laugh out loud (ha-ha)**
> **sing a song (la-la)**
> **shout "hurray" (hoo-ray)**

CANDELITA

This game is popular in almost every country under a different name. Children play this version in the Dominican Republic. Each one takes a place in a corner and along the wall in a room, or beside a bush out in the yard.

One person—"It"—is left without a place. "It" walks from child to child asking for a "Candelita" (a candle), and each one replies, "Ve a la otra esquinita" ("Go to the other corner").

While this is happening, the other members of the group try to exchange places. If "It" can catch an empty place, he or she is "safe." The one without the place is the new "It."

CALABAZA

In this Peruvian version of the same game, 5 children hold hands in the middle of the room, chanting:

**"Calabaza, calabaza—   "Pumpkin, pumpkin—
Cada uno a su casa!"   Each to his/her own house!"**

On the word "casa," they drop hands and run to a corner of the room. The child who is left out is "It." "It" goes from person to person asking:

"¿Tiene huevos?"   "Have you any eggs?"

And the game goes on as in "Candelita." If after a few tries, "It" has not captured a corner, start from the beginning with the chant, which is half the fun.

THE ALLEE ALLEE OH

There's a big ship sail-ing on the Al - lee Al - lee Oh, The Al - lee Al - lee Oh, the

Al - lee Al - lee Oh. There's a big ship sail - ing on the Al - lee Al - lee Oh,

Hey, the ding dong day.

There's a big ship sailing on the Allee Allee Oh,
The Allee Allee Oh, the Allee Allee Oh.
There's a big ship sailing on the Allee Allee Oh,
Hey, the ding dong day.

This English line dance needs a strong leader, but children as young as six can play and adults like it, too.

The leader of the line is called the Head and the person at the other end the Tail. The players in between take hands and don't let go for the rest of the game. The Tail places one hand flat against the wall, so the line is firmly anchored and cannot move too far.

Winding up

The Head leads the line over to the Tail, starting with a bouncing step. After everyone learns the game, the Head can lead with a run. The Tail and the person alongside the Tail lift their hands to form an arch. The Head leads the entire line under this arch. The person next to the Tail—instead of going under his or her own arm—makes only half a turn, faces the opposite direction from the rest of the line and just stands there with arms crossed.

THE ALLEE ALLEE OH

The Head continues to lead the line. This time it goes under the arch formed by the person who is turned half-way and the next person in line. This third person from the Tail turns half-way around (with arms crossed), and the line continues under the arches. The Tail remains with arms straight, still holding onto the wall. By the time all the players have made the half-turn and have their arms crossed, the line is all wound up and you have reached the middle of the game.

Unwinding

The person who is next to the Head starts the unwinding process by pulling his or her head under the arms. That player faces front now with arms uncrossed. The next person pulls the two unwound players under, and the unwinding continues until the line is back to its original position.

Sing the song loud and clear all the while.

RATTLESNAKE

Number of players: 12 - 20

R - A - T - T - L - E - S - N - A - K -

E spells Rat-tle-snake!

R-A-T-T-L-E
S-N-A-K-E
spells Rattlesnake!

This is an American version of "The Allee Allee Oh." The action is the same during the first part, when you wind up. But when the winding is complete, the Tail and the Head *both* turn half-way around, cross their arms, and move near each other to join hands.

Now the line is a tight circle. Each player is facing away from the circle center, holding on with crossed arms. The entire circle jumps up and down together, singing one more verse in almost a yell. Then the circle falls apart with lots of laughing and the game is over.

ANGEL AND DEVIL (Tug-of-War)

This great tug-of-war comes from South America. Choose an angel and a devil. Each one stands in a corner of the room. The rest of the players line up behind a leader. The leader walks down the line and whispers the name of a different fruit in each player's ear.

Now the game is ready to start. The angel moves to the leader and knocks on the floor or on the wall, saying:

ANGEL:	Tūn, tūn.	Knock, knock.
LEADER:	¿Quién es?	Who's there?
ANGEL:	El ángel con la bola de oro.	The angel with the ball of gold.
LEADER:	¿Qué desea?	What do you want?
ANGEL:	Una fruta.	A fruit.
LEADER:	¿Qué fruta?	Which fruit?
ANGEL:	Plátano.	Banana.
LEADER:	Sí tengo. (or) No tengo.	I've got one. (or) I haven't got any.

If one of the players has the name of the fruit, he or she goes to the angel's corner. If not, the angel retires to its corner alone. Now the devil steps forward and says:

DEVIL:	Tūn, tūn.	Knock, knock.
LEADER:	¿Quién es?	Who's there?
DEVIL:	El diablo de los diez mille cuernos.	The devil with 10,000 horns.
LEADER:	(repeat as before)	

Repeat the same dialogue with the angel and devil alternating turns until all the players have been chosen to be on the side of the angel or the devil. Then the groups line up on either side of a center line (draw it with chalk, if you're outside, or use a string or a ribbon). Each child holds onto the waist of the child in front. There is no way to predict beforehand how the lines will turn out—equal or unequal—which adds to the fun. The two lines face each other and the angel and devil lock hands. The leader yells "FRUTA!" and the two lines begin a tug-of-war. The line that pulls the other group over the center line wins, be it angel or devil!

Choose a new leader, angel and devil from the winning group and start the game again.

Exotic fruta:

Try to avoid apples and oranges and get on to more exotic fruits—avocadoes, limes, figs and kumquats; olives, persimmons and loquats; pomegranates and dates. Don't forget the berries: blackberries, loganberries, huckleberries, boysenberries, cranberries, gooseberries, as well as raspberries, strawberries and blueberries.

Variations:

You don't need to limit this game to fruits. Try using vegetables, colors, trees, countries, dogs, desserts, monsters, any category you like.

ICE CREAM TRAIN (Yesh Li Gleeda)

Yesh li glee-da a-chi to-va, Glee-da met-zu-ya-na, Knu mi-me-ny ye-la-dim!

Glee-da to-va, glee-da to-va!

Yesh li gleeda achí tova,
Gleeda metzuyana,
Knu mimeny yeladim!
Gleeda tova, gleeda tova!

I have the very
best ice cream,
Wonderful ice cream,
Buy from me, children!
Great ice cream,
great ice cream!

This delightful Israeli game is a tribute to ice cream. Sing it in a light, sprightly way, with words short, sharp and clear. If the foreign words are too difficult, sing "la, la, la," or the English words.

One person walks around the center of the circle, while the others sing and clap in place until the end of the third line. On "yeladim," the center person faces someone in the circle and they become partners. On the next word, "Gleeda," the partners put right hands on their foreheads (palms out) and left hands on their hips (fingers facing back and palms turned out). Their right heels are forward and their bodies lean naturally to the right side.

On the next word, "tova," they jump into the same position with the other hand on forehead and waist and the body leaning the other way. This sequence repeats when the words "Gleeda tova" repeat, so the movement is really done 4 times, twice on each side.

The person in the center turns and the partner holds his or her waist. The song starts again. With light, bouncing steps, the "ice cream train" wends its way around the inside of the circle until the word "yeladim," when the train faces a new partner. All 3 players do the "Gleeda tova" step.

Now the line turns around so that the second player becomes the leader and the newest player is at the end. The next time the dance repeats, the line turns around again so that the person who was at the tail will be at the head. The dance goes on until everyone is aboard.

Long trains:

If the group is very large, start with 2 players in the center, each choosing partners at the same time, so that you have 2 ice cream trains in the circle. The trains don't need to go in the same direction; they can weave their own patterns.

JIGSAW SONGS

Number of players: Unlimited

Each time you sing these songs, you leave out another part until barely a shell is left. Then put the pieces back and sing the song again. It's like breaking apart and re-building your own jigsaw puzzle.

John Brown's Baby

John Brow-n's ba - by had a cold up-on his chest, John Brow-n's ba - by had a

cold up - on his chest. John Brow - n's ba - by had a cold up - on his chest, and they

rubbed it in with cam-phor-a - ted oil.

John Brown's_____ had a_____ upon his_____,
     (rock)   (cough)   (tap)

John Brown's_____ had a_____upon his_____,
     (rock)   (cough)   (tap)

John Brown's_____ had a_____upon his_____,
     (rock)   (cough)   (tap)

And they_____with_____ .
     (rubbed it in)   (hold nose)

First sing the song without motions. The second time leave out the word "baby" in every line. Make believe you're rocking a baby in your arms instead. The third time, in addition to "baby," leave out "cold" in each line. Sneeze or cough and shake your head, instead. The fourth time, besides "baby" and "cold," tap your chest with a loud thud instead of saying "chest." The fifth time you leave out "rubbed it in" and rub your chest in a circle instead. Finally, for "camphorated oil," hold your nose and make a face (it smells bad).

JIGSAW SONGS

And Eyes and Ears and Mouth and Nose

Sing this silly song to the tune of "There Is a Tavern in the Town." First sing it through once. As you mention each body part, point to it. The second time around, don't sing the word "head." Just point to it and sing the other words. Stick to the original rhythm even though you're leaving out words. Third time eliminate "Head and shoulders;" the fourth time "Head and shoulders, knees;" and the fifth time "Head and shoulders, knees and toes." Sing "And eyes and ears

and mouth and nose" twice as loud, to make up for the quiet parts. Increase your speed each time until the song really flies.

Group Eyes and Ears

Divide into 4 groups: one is Head, one Shoulders, another Knees, the last Toes. Try interesting patterns: each group can jump on its word, for example, or jump and turn. The possibilities are endless.

ROUNDS

Number of players: Unlimited

Rounds are fun to sing, whether you're in a group or alone with a friend. They are especially good around a campfire, and when you have no piano or other instrument, since they have their own built-in accompaniment. When several parts mingle and pass through each other in different rhythms and with different melodies, the sound has a rich fullness which a single tune never can have.

Divide the group into 2 or 3 parts. After Group 1 sings the first 2 measures, the second group starts to sing. This is indicated in the music by a *. If you have a third group, they start when Group 2 has completed the first 2 measures. Decide beforehand how many times you will sing the song through. Each group will, of course, finish at a different time, and the sound will diminish gradually, until only one group ends the song.

It is a good idea to choose one person to be the conductor, who signals to the groups when to come in and fade out. The conductor can use his or her hands or a baton.

Come Follow

Come fol - low, fol - low, fol - low, fol - low, fol - low, fol - low me.

*Whith-er shall I fol - low, fol - low, fol - low? Whith-er shall I fol - low, fol - low thee?

To the green - wood, to the green - wood, to the green - wood, green - wood tree.

26

ROUNDS

Scotland's Burning

Scot-land's burn-ing, Scot-land's burn-ing, *Look yon-der, Look yon-der, Fi-re, fi-re, fi-re,

fi-re, But we have no wa-ter!

This round is a slow, nostalgic one. Sing it smoothly and tenderly. Try it with 4 groups, each one coming in after the previous group sings one line.

Vent Frais (Cool Wind)

Vent frais, vent du ma-tin, *Sous le vent le sommeil des mont-agnes,

Joie du vent qui passe — A-llons dans le grand...

which means
Cool wind, wind of the morn
Under the wind the sleeping mountains lie,
Joyous wind that blows; let's run in the great ...

This round has two very different versions different in feeling and language, even though you sing them both to the same tune.

Hi-Ho

Hi-ho,
Nobody home.
Meat nor drink nor money
Have I none.
Yet will I be me-e-e-ery ...

HANDS, KNEES AND BOOMS-A-DAISIE

Waltz Tempo

Hands, knees and booms - a - dai - sie — I like a bus - tle that bends._____

Hands, knees and booms - a - dai - sie — What is a bump be-tween friends?_____

Hands, knees and booms - a - dai - sie — Turn to your part - ner and bow._____

Hands, knees and booms - a - dai - sie — Let's make this par - ty a wow — Bow-wow!

HANDS, KNEES AND BOOMS-A-DAISIE

This dancing game is easy and a good ice-breaker. You do it with partners, either in a long straight line with partners facing each other, or in a circle, with one partner's back towards the circle center.

Hands, knees and booms-a-daisie—

Whenever you sing this line, clap your hands on the first word. On the second word, bend and put your hands on your knees. On the third word, straighten up, turn and bump bottoms with your partner sideways.

I like a bustle that bends.

Face your partner. Put your hands on your hips and move your hips from side to side 4 times.

Hands, knees and booms-a-daisie—
What is a bump between friends?

Repeat these movements.

Hands, knees and booms-a-daisie—

Repeat the clap-knee-and-bottom-bump movement.

Turn to your partner and bow—

Turn once around in place. Girls curtsy. Boys place one hand in front of the waist, one hand behind and bend low, keeping legs straight.

Hands, knees and booms-a-daisie—

Repeat the clap-knee-and-bottom-bump movement.

Let's make this party a wow—

Put your hands on your hips and move your hips from side to side 3 times.

Bow-wow!

Partners move close to each other. Boys stretch their arms out around and behind the girls' waists. Girls stretch their arms behind the boys' necks; both clap hands twice.

The line or circle now moves down one, so that each person has a new partner.

CRUSHED PEPPERS (Vibersko)

This fast line dance comes from Prizren, a Serbian part of Yugoslavia. It is one of many line dances which are called "kolos," and it is wonderful fun.

Take hands and form a line. First you do the chorus step and then you crush the peppers.

Chorus Step

The chorus step is a bouncy walk: step out on your right foot and bend your knee. Give each step 2 counts—step and bend. Do 24 of these step-and-bends, as the circle moves to the right. There is a pause in the music when the chorus is over.

Pepper-Crushing

Each time you crush the peppers you do it with a different part of your body. The first 2 times you crush the peppers, keep holding hands in the line. The third, fourth and fifth times, drop hands. You need them for the movement. After each pepper-crushing, pause and then start the chorus again.

Crushed peppers 1:

Tap your right foot in place 12 times.

Crushed peppers 2:

Kneel, left leg in front, right knee on the floor. Tap 12 times on the floor with your right knee and rise.

Crushed peppers 3:

Kneel on both knees. Put your left hand on the floor in front of you, lean forward, and tap 12 times in front with your right elbow. Stand.

Crushed peppers 4:

Down on both knees, bend forward and tap your forehead to the floor 12 times. Stand.

Crushed peppers 5:

Sit on the floor. Lean on your hands and tap your bottom 12 times on the floor. Finish in the same sitting position, but with your hands palms down on your thighs.

The 12 taps represent the crushing of the peppers, so as you do it, you may want to say:

> **Crush with your foot.**
> **Crush with your knee.**
> **Crush with your elbow.**
> **Crush with your forehead.**
> **Crush with your bottom.**

Keep your body straight and tight while you walk and use strong movements on the crushing of the peppers. Keep the line moving and don't wait too long between the chorus and the crushing.

CRUSHED PEPPERS (Vibersko)

Strong and staccato

Chorus

Number of players: 8 - Unlimited

Pepper-crushing

(Pause)

Crushed Peppers Deluxe:

For a more difficult (and more interesting) dance, use the hora step instead of a simple bounce-walk for the chorus. The hora step consists of 4 separate moves:

1. Step and bend with your right foot to the right side.

2. Cross your left foot in front of the right, step and bend.

3. Step to the right and swing left foot across right.

4. Step to the left and bend and swing your right foot across.

   If you're full of energy, add a hop on steps 3 and 4 on the standing foot.

31

LOVE GROWS UNDER THE WILD OAK TREE

VERSE

Love grows
under the
wild oak
tree.
Sugar
melts like
can-
dy,
Top of the
mountain
shines like
gold, and you
kiss your little
feller (sweetie) sort of
han-
dy.

CHORUS

Dreams
dreams,
sweet
dreams
under the
wild oak
tree-
eee.
Dreams,
dreams,
sweet
dreams,
one for
you and
me.
Oh!

This is one of the great finger-snapping, clapping and tapping games, and you can do it by yourself, with a friend, or in a whole circle of people.

Love grows   **Dreams**

Bend your knees a little and slap your thighs twice.

under the   **dreams,**

Straighten up and clap your hands twice.

wild oak   **sweet**

Stretch both arms out to the side, palms flat and facing out, fingers pointing up. If you are in a circle, clap hands with the people next to you (on either side).

tree.   **dreams**

Cross your arms over your chest and slap your shoulders twice.

Sugar melts like   **under the wild oak**

Bend your elbows outward, so that your hands are close to the middle of your chest. Move your hands over and around each other and wiggle your fingers, so it feels like sugar melting.

candy,   **tree-eee.**

Snap fingers of both hands over your right shoulder, looking over your right shoulder at the same time on the "can," and snap and look over your left shoulder on the "dy."

Top of the mountain   **Dreams, dreams,**

Same movements as for "Love grows under the."

shines like gold, and you   **sweet dreams,**

Same movements as for "wild oak tree."

kiss your little feller sort of   **one for you and**

Same movements as for "sugar melts like."

handy.   **me. Oh!**

Same movements as for "candy," but to the left side.

Do all of these movements as you sing first the verse, then the chorus and then the verse again. After you

LOVE GROWS UNDER THE WILD OAK TREE

Number of players: Unlimited

Love grows un - der the wild oak tree. Su - gar melts like can - dy,

Top of the moun - tain shines like gold, And you kiss your lit - tle fel - ler sort of hand - y.

Dreams, dreams, sweet dreams, Un - der the wild oak tree - eee.

Dreams, dreams, sweet dreams, one for you and me. Oh!

perform them a few times, they become automatic and you can do them with eyes closed (which is fun). Try speeding up the music, which also means speeding up the movements. Go fast enough and it can end in total chaos!

Wild Oak Duet

Divide the group in two, with one group singing the verse at the same time as the other group sings the chorus. It is a beautiful duet. Movements are the same.

RUMBLE TO THE BOTTOM

Number of players: 10 - 25

Oh, we're going to the circus, We're going to the fair To see the señ-or-i-ta With the flow-ers in her hair.

Oh, we're going to the circus,
We're going to the fair
To see the señorita
With the flowers in her hair.

Oh, shake it, shake it, shake it,
Shake it if you can,
Shake it like a milkshake,
And do the best you can.

Oh, rumble to the bottom,
And rumble to the top.
Turn around and turn around
Until you make a stop!

This inner city game from Puerto Rico is always popular because it combines a traditional circle dance with just about anything you want!

"It" stands in the middle, while the rest of the players form a circle around her or him. On the first stanza the circle walks around clockwise.

During the second stanza, the players shake themselves all over (shoulders and hips included). They can do whatever dance is "in," instead, if they prefer.

On the first 2 lines of the third stanza, the dancers in the circle stop. They watch "It," who keeps shaking, but this time does it while sinking lower and lower until almost down on the floor. Then "It" shakes all the way up again.

On the last 2 lines, "It" stretches out one hand in front in a fist, pointing the index finger. "It" covers his or her eyes with the other hand, and spins around until the song stops. Whichever player the finger points to at the end of the song is the next "It."

DRAGON (Ular Naga)

U - lar na - ga pan - djang - nja bu - kah ke - pa - lang.

Men - dja-lar -dja - lar se-la - lu ki - an ke - ma - ri. Um - pan jang le - zat - i - tu -

- lah di - tja - ri, I - ni-di - a - nja jang ter-be - la - kang.

Ular naga pan-djang-nja bu-kah ke-pa-lang.
Men-dja-lar-dja-lar se-la-lu ki-an ke-ma-ri.
Um-pan jang le-zat-i-tu-lah di-tja-ri,
I-ni-di-a-nja jang ter-be-la-kang.

means

See the dragon long and fierce
Terrible is he.
Here and there he twists and turns
As you all can see.
Prey that's good to eat he seems to lack.
Here he's found it too, at the very back.

This musical game is played in China, where it is called "Catching the Dragon's Tail," and in Indonesia. Here is a version from west Java.

The players stand in a line, single file, each holding onto the waist of the child in front. They walk in time with the music as they sing the song. When the song is finished, the first person on line, who is the Head of the dragon, tries to tag the last person, who is the Tail.

This is not as easy as it sounds; it requires skill, quick perception and an awareness of the group's mobility. The Tail tries to escape. If the line breaks, the game must start again. When the Head catches the Tail, the Tail moves to the front of the line and becomes the new Head, and everyone moves one down the line.

This is a strenuous and intense game. Don't play it more than two or three times!

Reprinted by permission of the U.S. Committee for UNICEF. Translation by Francine Wickes.

I WANNA BE A FRIEND OF YOURS

I wan-na be a friend of yours, mmmm and a lit-tle bit more.

I wan-na be a pal of yours, mmmm and a lit-tle bit more. I wan-na be a

bum - ble bee, buz - zing round your door. I wan-na mean a lot to you,

mmmm and a lit-tle bit, mmmm and a lit-tle bit, mmmm and a whole lot more!

I WANNA BE A FRIEND OF YOURS

I wanna be a friend of yours, mmmm and a little bit more.
I wanna be a pal of yours, mmmm and a little bit more.
I wanna be a bumble bee,
Buzzing round your door.
I wanna mean a lot to you,
Mmmm and a little bit, mmmm and a little bit
Mmmm and a whole lot more.

Oh, you are a friend of mine, mmmm and a little bit more.
You are a pal of mine, mmmm and a little bit more.
You are a bumble bee,
Buzzing round my door.
You mean a lot to me
Mmmm and a little bit,
Mmmm and a little bit,
Mmmm and a whole lot more!

This circle dance requires a great deal of concentration, but it is worth the effort. The only thing you need to know is how to count up to 8.

Take hands in a circle. As you sing the first line of the song, slide 8 counts to the left around the circle. On the second line, reverse direction and slide 8 to the right. On the third line of the song, "I wanna be a bumble bee," slide 4 to the left; on the fourth line, 4 to the right.

Now the dance speeds up. On line 5, slide 2 to the left and 2 to the right. On line 6, slide 1 left, 1 right, 1 left, 1 right (almost a leap from one foot to the other). On the last line, walk 3 counts into the circle. On the last count, stamp loudly and put your arms around the shoulders of the people beside you. Hug them hard.

This dance is exhausting. Take a couple of minutes to catch your breath after you finish the first stanza, but don't drop hands. Just walk back to your starting place, take a few deep breaths, and you are ready to start the second stanza.

The rhythms and movements of this dance are easier to remember than they seem to be at first.

The slides go like this:
8–8
4–4
2-2
1-1
1-1
3 steps in and stamp

Follow the counts carefully. This is an exact dance. If you don't do it precisely, the group falls apart. The quick changes of direction in the dance are particularly tricky. You need to think about putting on the brakes before you finish each set of slides, so that you're ready to go the other way at the end of the line.

With Large Groups:

You can do this dance in a number of interesting ways. A large group can form two circles, one separately or one inside the other. Each circle does one line of the song and then rests. The other circle repeats their movements, like an echo. As a finale, both circles do the entire dance together at the same time. If the circles are one inside the other (the inner circle is smaller), the inside circle starts sliding to the right, so that the circles go in opposite directions.

MYAN MYAN

Number of players: 6 - 15

Myan myan pay jah bah oh may sway ah paun doh, myan myan
pay jah bah, ma pay nine yin pyin twet.

Myan myan
Pay jah bah oh
May sway ah paun doh,
Myan myan
Pay jah bah,
Ma pay nine
Yin pyin twet.

means

Give or pass quickly, friends,
Give it quickly.
If you can't do it,
Then go out.

In this Burmese game, everyone sits in a circle. Each person holds a small object—like a smooth stone—or a nut. First, to get the rhythm of the song, tap the stone in front of you on the underlined word. When you come to the words, "Ma pay nine" hold it still, and then tap again on the last word, "twet."

This is only the preparation for the game; now you're ready to play. As you sing the song again, instead of tapping the stone on the underlined words, pass it to the person on your left and receive a stone from the person on your right. When you come to the words, "Ma pay nine," hold the stone. Then pass it again on "twet." If you forget to hold the stone at the right time, or if you fumble with it, you are out. To make the game more exciting, speed up the tempo each time you sing the song. The last person left is the winner.

Myan Without Words:

Instead of saying the words, you can sing la-la-la, or hum the music or whistle it. Also try the game in silence, so that you hear only the rhythm of the stones as they are passed. You'll still need to sing it to yourself so that you know when to hold still and when to pass it along.

Reprinted by permission of the U.S. Committee for UNICEF.

ECHUNGA PARA LA YUNGA

Lyrically

Es - ta e - ra una ni - ñi - ta, Gra - ci - o - sa y muy bo - ni - ta, que
(Es - te e - ra un ni - ñi - to, Gra - ci - o - so y muy bo - ni - to,)

cuan - do pe - dí - a a - gua, se e - cha - ba a za - pa - tear. E - chun - ga pa - ra la

Speed it up

yun - ga — e - chun - ga pa - ra la yá — e - chun - ga pa - ra la yun - ga — e - chun - ga pa - ra la yá.

This Peruvian circle dance can go on endlessly—or until everyone has had a turn.

Start by forming a circle and choose one person, "It," to go into the center. The children walk around the circle singing the verse, which means:

There was a little girl (boy),
Charming and very pretty (handsome),
When she (he) would ask for water,
She (he) would stamp down with her (his) foot.

"It" faces someone in the circle. With hands on hips, "It" jumps and extends the right foot—heel first—then the left foot—and the right, again—in a 1-2-3-Stop rhythm. As "It" repeats this step, he or she sings the nonsense verse:

Echunga para la yunga—
Echunga para la yá—
Echunga para la yunga—
Echunga para la yá.

Whoever was chosen takes the place in the center of the circle as the new "It," and the song repeats.

CAROUSEL

Pret - ty maid - en, sweet and fair, Car - ou - sel is run - ning.

It will run till eve - ning: Lit - tle ones a nick - el, Big ones a dime. Hur - ry

up! Get a mate! Or you'll sure - ly be too late! Ha, ha, ha!

Hap - py are we — An - der - son and Hen - der - son and Pe - ter - son and Me!

CAROUSEL

Pretty <u>maiden</u>, <u>sweet</u> and <u>fair</u>,
<u>Carousel</u> is <u>running</u>.
<u>It</u> will <u>run</u> till <u>evening</u>:
<u>Little</u> <u>ones</u> a <u>nickel</u>,
<u>Big</u> ones a <u>dime</u>.
Hurry up! Get a mate!
Or you'll surely be too late!

Ha, ha, ha!
Happy are we—
Anderson and Henderson
And Peterson and Me!

Ha, ha, ha!
Happy are we—
Anderson and Henderson
And Peterson and Me!

This Swedish dance starts quietly as a carousel does, and builds in intensity until—near the end—you have to hold on tight or you fly up in the air.

Choose partners, who stand in a circle, one behind the other, facing the circle center. The inner circle joins hands, and the children in the outer circle place their hands on their partners' shoulders.

As the dance starts, the people in the inner circle rise up on their toes. Their partners bend their knees (in place). Then they reverse: the inner circle people bend their knees while their partners rise up, so that you get the up-and-down feeling of the horses in a carousel. Make the change on the underlined words until you reach "Hurry up." Then everyone stops and stamps in place until the end of the first stanza, "Or you'll surely be too late!"

In the second stanza, the carousel takes off. Both circles slide quickly (double-time) to the left. Partners hold on tight, and the circles seem to spend more time in the air than on the ground! The inner circle (which is smaller) must take small steps. The outer circle has the more difficult task of taking large steps to draw the bigger circumference. Eight slides should get both circles through the stanza.

When you repeat this stanza, try to speed up even more, sliding in the same direction, for a total of 16 slides. The second time you do the dance, change places with your partner.

This dance requires awareness of your partner and the other dancers around you, too. Each person is directly involved in the success of the circle and the dance as a whole. Sing the first part softly and let the song get more and more frantic, until you almost shout the last section.

Different rides

Both partners can rise and bend in the same direction for the first stanza, at the same time. Or count off couples in each circle as 1 and 2, so that all the 1's rise as the 2's bend. If you want a greater challenge, continue with the rises and bends, but also take little steps to the left on the words, "Little ones a nickel, Big ones a dime," then stamp as before, and slide.

HOYA-HOYE

The Ethiopian New Year falls on September 11th. After sunset on New Year's Eve, groups of small boys walk through their village carrying torches and serenading each house. Their song has 3 parts. In the first 2 parts of this version, you chant the words. Here they are in Amharic, Ethiopia's official language. Pronounce them just the way they look, stressing each syllable equally.

Part 1:

Hoya-hoye, hoya-hoye,
Yene mebet atiwhichi gwaro.
Ainish yaberal inde korkoro.
Hoya-hoye, gude,
Dabo dabo yilal hode.

Ishim ahnd nuhw.
Imbim ahnd nuhw.
Iguada gebto zimu mindinuhw.
Hoya-hoye, gude,
Dabo dabo yilal hode.

which means

Hoya-hoye, hoya-hoye,
Mistress, don't go into your back-yard.
Your eyes shine like the sun from a tin roof.
Hoya-hoye, I have a secret,
My tummy wants bread.

Yes is an answer.
No is also an answer.
But staying indoors in silence is no answer.
Hoya-hoye, I have a secret,
My tummy wants bread.

The women of the house give the boys freshly baked bread and rolls after this first part. The leader of the boys thanks them in the second part:

Part 2:

Weldew yikoyun kebdew,
Lamet wend lij weldew,
Keguaro tija asrew,
Weldew yikoyun kebdew.

which means

When we come back a year from now,
May you be blessed with a son,
And a calf tied in your back-yard,
When we come back a year from now.

All the boys sing the third part, which is a haunting song. The word "digemena" repeats throughout the verse—it means "once more." While one group of boys sings the other words of the song, the second group echoes "Digemena." Try using the original words. They are fun to say and easy to sing.

HOYA-HOYE

Number of players: Unlimited

A - met lau - da - met, Di - ge - me - na. A - met Di - ge - me - na Ye - ma - mi - yen bat-eh Di -
- ge - me - na, A - met Di - ge - me - na Ya - ba - bi - yen bat-eh Di - ge - me - na, A - met Di - ge - me - na.

Part 3:

First Group Sings:	Second Group Sings:		
Amet laudamet,	Digemena.		Next year on this holiday
Amet	Digemena		May God allow us to come,	Once more.
Yemamiyen bateh	Digemena,	which means	Next year	Once more
Amet	Digemena		To our Mother's house	Once more,
Yababiyen bateh	Digemena,		Next year	Once more
Amet	Digemena.		To our Father's house	Once more,
			Next year	Once more.

"Our Mother's house" and "our Father's house" refer to every house. In Ethiopian villages, every man was considered the father of the village children and every woman their mother.

43

SQUARE DANCES

Go into the Kitchen and Take a Peek

Number of players: Sets of 8

Go in-to the kitch-en and take a peek, Back to the cen-ter and

swing your sweet. Go in-to the kitch-en and swing once more. Go back to the cen-ter and swing all four.

On to the next!

Set up a square with 4 couples (gent on the left and lady on the right), 2 couples facing each other, each couple forming a side of the square. The couple which starts the dance is the one with its back to the instrument (or machine) playing the music.

1
Go into the kitchen

The first couple walks to the couple on its right. The first gent stands near the second lady, and the first lady near the second gent.

2
And take a peek

On the word "peek," the first couple jumps alongside the second couple, leans over behind them and peeks at each other.

3
Back to the center and swing your sweet

They immediately go back to the center. Children under 8 take hands and skip around each other. Over 8-years-old, they swing their partners.

44

4
Into the kitchen and peek once more

The first couple repeats the sequence, but this time they jump and peek on the word "more."

5
Go back to the center and swing all four.

The first and second couple both swing (or skip with) their own partners. The first couple must return to the center before they swing, which won't give them time to go more than once around.

6
On to the next!

Now the first couple walks to the third couple and the dance repeats.

7

When the first couple has danced with each of the 3 couples, call "Everybody swing" or "Promenade around the ring" or "Honor your partners" (see page 49).

Now the second couple walks out to the third couple and the dance starts again. Each couple takes its turn leading the dance with the other couples. Between each sequence, add extra calls, as in Step 7, and finish with one of these:

Take your honey to a nice soft chair.
You know where and I don't care.

Swing your partner, don't be afraid,
Take your honey and all promenade.

Meet your honey, give her a swing.
Swing 'em all around the ring.
Up on the toe, down on the heel,
The harder you swing, the better they feel.

Meet your own, remember the call,
Swing your own and promenade all.

Circle all 8 hands around—
Right foot up and left foot down.

Circle left and places all,
Swing your honey and don't you fall!

Swing her high and swing her low,
Swing that gal in calico.
Swing that darling little miss,
Give her a hug, but not a kiss.

The Swing: partners put right feet near each other, hold arms in a really stretched-out dance position and look at each other over their right shoulders. They then pivot around with the left foot, keeping the right foot pretty much in place.

SQUARE DANCES

The Lady Round The Lady

Set up the square with 4 couples. Count off the couples: the first or "head" couple, is the one with its back to the music. The couple to the right of the head couple is Couple 2 and so on to Couple 4.

I
Oh, it's—the—lady round the lady
and the gent around the gent,

The head couple moves to Couple 2 and walks between them. Couple 2 should take a step away from each other to let the head couple through. Just as the call says, the lady of the head couple circles the lady of Couple 2, while the gent of the head couple circles the #2 gent. The head couple comes back to face Couple 2 again.

2
And the gent around the lady
And the lady round the gent,

The head lady circles the #2 gent while the head gent goes around the #2 lady.

3
Four hands round, circle to the left

When the head couple finishes circling, they go back to face the second couple again. All now join hands and circle to the left.

4
Swing your partner once around
and on to the next.

Both sets of partners swing. The head couple moves on to Couple 3 and the dance repeats.

5
When the head couple finishes the same sequence with Couple 3, they go on to Couple 4. When the dance is complete, use a general call such as:

6
Comb your hair and button your shoe,
Promenade like you always do.

Partners face counter-clockwise, join right hands and then left hands, and walk or skip around the circle until they get back to their original places.

Now it is time for Couple 2 to lead off and repeat the dance, with the third, fourth and head couple, and the dance continues until each couple has taken the lead.

Double Couple:

For a quicker dance, Couples 1 and 3 dance at the same time; the head couple going out to Couple 2, and Couple 3 going out to Couple 4. Then do a promenade or a swing-your-partner (partners can just hold hands and skip around each other). When the first sequence is complete, Couple 2 goes to Couple 3, and Couple 4 goes to the head couple.

SQUARE DANCES

The Lady Round The Lady

Oh, it's the la - dy round the la - dy and the gent a - round the gent, And the

gent a - round the la - dy and the la - dy round the gent, Four hands round,

cir - cle to the left, Swing your part - ner once a - round and on to the next.

Changing the Calls:

For variety, try these:

The sheep around the sheep
And the wolf around the wolf,

or
The cat around the cat,
And the dog around the dog.

Or try any other combination of animals that relate to each other, such as lion and tiger, porpoise and whale. Everything works.

SQUARE DANCES

Square Dance in the Round

48

SQUARE DANCES

Square Dance in the Round

1
First you whistle, then you sing,
All join hands and form a ring.

Form a circle, gents on the left-hand side of their ladies.

2
Circle to the left,
The other way back—
You're on the wrong track.

The circle moves to the left with a walking step, a skipping step, or a 1-2-3-hop step. At the call "The other way back, you're on the wrong track," the circle switches direction and moves to the right with the same step.

3
Honor your corner, lady,
Honor your partners all.

Turn to your corner (the person next to you—but not your partner); ladies curtsy and gents bow. Then do the same with your partner.

4
Swing your little partner round
And promenade the hall.
Ice-cream and lemonade,
If you will only promenade.

Children age 8 or under skip around each other. Over age 8, partners swing (see explanation on page 45). Then all promenade (page 50).

5
Back to your places.

Partners face counterclockwise, give each other right hands, then left hands, skip once around and back to their place.

6
One big circle.
Gents to the center and form a right-hand star.
Right hand out, left hand back
Make your feet go wickety-wack.

Form one circle again. Then gents walk to the circle center with their right hands extended, left hands behind their backs. They put their right hands into the hub of the circle, one on top of the other. Then they face left and walk around once.

7
Meet your partner, say "Hello,"
Hold her tight and away you go.

When the gents circle back to their partners, they say "Hello," without taking their right hands out of the circle. They hold their ladies' waists with their left hands. The ladies put their right arms around the gents' waists and walk with them once more around. Ladies put their left hands on their hips for this turn, or hold out their skirts.

Square Dance in the Round (continued)

8

Turn and make a left-hand star.

Everyone changes direction. The men put their left hands into the circle center to form another star. The ladies hold onto the gents' waists with their left hands. Gents hold their ladies' waists with the right hands, and the circle walks counterclockwise and back to their place. Then they form a circle again.

9

All join hands and jump up high,
Keep on jumping till you reach the sky.

The entire circle jumps in place, holding hands.

10

Do-si-do with your corner,
With your corner do-si-do.
Do-si-do with your partner,
Oh, why are you so slow?

Face your corner, cross your arms in front of you, shoulder high and walk or skip towards your corner. Pass right shoulders and go around each other, but keep facing the same direction. Now pass left shoulders and come back to place, so that you haven't turned around at all. Then do the same step with your own partner.

11

Allemande left with your corner,
Right hand to your partner
And a grand right and left around the hall.
When you meet your own,
You promenade her home!

Give your corner your left hand and walk or skip once around and back to place. Now give your partner your right hand and walk past him or her, passing right shoulders. Now drop that hand, and continue in the same direction (ladies go clockwise, gents counterclockwise), giving your left hand to the next person you meet. Pass him (or her) by, and give your right hand to the next person, left to the next, and so on. When you meet your own partner, promenade home.

TEA AND RICE

Perky

This folk dance from Israel is action fun for everyone, from second-graders to adults.

You need groups of 3—like sandwiches—two pieces of bread on the outside and cheese in between. Each group holds hands and faces counterclockwise, to form a spoke coming from the circle center. Give each player a letter: the one nearest the center of the circle is A (bread), the one in the middle is B (cheese), the one on the outer edge of the circle is C (bread). Make sure everyone knows his or her letter.

Measures 1 and 2: Each group takes 8 small step-hops, starting on the left foot and moving counterclockwise in the circle.

Measures 3 and 4: Each group of 3 (still holding hands and facing counterclockwise) takes $3\frac{1}{2}$ slides towards the circle center—slide-together, slide-together, slide-together, step-and-stop. Then they repeat the sliding movement away from the circle center; A leads the line in and C leads the line out.

Measures 5 and 6: Each line of 3 turns and faces the circle center. A leads the line. All bend down low and take 4 steps, clapping down low on each step. Then immediately they turn half-way around and C leads the line out, taking 4 steps and lifting the body and clapping high.

Measure 7: A, B and C take hands again in their original positions. They move 4 steps forward.

Measure 8: A and C (still holding hands with B) swing their arms back. When they swing them forward again, they also swing B out of their group! B goes into the group in front, while the B from the group behind swings into their group.

The dance repeats with the new B in each group. It's a good idea to change parts, so that everyone has a chance to be B.

TROIKA

A troika is a Russian sleigh drawn by 3 horses, and it is sets of 3 "horses" who perform this exuberant dance.

The 3 horses line up side by side, close to each other, holding hands and lifting them up in the air, as if they are hitched to the sleigh with a high harness. All the horses, in sets of 3, form a long line.

Measures 1-4: The horses run forward 8 steps, lifting their knees up high in a kind of prance. Then they take 8 prancing steps back to where they started, still lifting their knees high in front, even though they are going backwards.

Measures 5 and 6: The 2 horses on the left (let's call them A and B), still holding hands, raise their arms in the air to form an arch. The horse on the right (C) runs 8 steps under the arch and back to place, pulling B under the arch, too. A takes running steps in place. (In a fancier version, A can turn under his or her own arm.)

Measures 7 and 8: Repeat the same step as in the previous 2 measures, but this time B and C form the arch and A runs under it, pulling B along. C runs in place. Then all 3 horses form a circle.

Measures 9-11: The horses take 12 running steps to the left, pulling away from each other.

Measure 12: They stamp 3 times, hard, in place and pause.

Measures 13-15: They reverse and run 12 counts in the opposite direction.

Measure 16: They stamp 3 times, straighten out the line on the last count, and are ready to start the dance again.

Since there is so much running, this is a tiring dance (good for rainy days), but most "horses" want to repeat it several times.

TROIKA

Tougher Troikas:

For a more difficult troika, the trios can dance in a different formation—still in groups of 3, but in short lines coming out from the center of the circle, like the spokes of a wheel. The horses on the outer edge of the circle need to take larger steps in order to keep the line straight. If you want to use the dance as a mixer, on the final stamp, shoot the middle horse (B) into the next set (see "Tea and Rice").

CHUN-GUM (Chewing Gum)

This song originated on the streets of New York in the early part of this century which accounts for the grammatical errors and mispronunciations in the verse.

My mamma gave me a penny
To buy some candy.
I didn't buy no candy,
I bought some chun gum.

CHORUS
Chu chu chu chu chu chun-gum
Chu chu chu chun-gum
I didn't buy no candy (pickle, etc.)
I bought some chun-gum.

My mamma gave me a nickel
To buy a pickle.
I didn't buy no pickle,
I bought some chun-gum.

CHORUS

My mamma gave me ten cents,
I shouldn't wet my new pants.
I didn't wet my new pants,
I bought some chun-gum.

CHORUS

My mamma gave me a quarter,
I shouldn't go in the water.
I didn't go in the water,
I bought some chun-gum.

CHORUS

My mamma gave me a dollar,
I didn't shouldn't holler.
I didn't shouldn't holler,
I bought some chun-gum.

This lively street song has easy movements to go with it.

Form a circle and walk or skip clockwise (to the left), starting with the right foot. Swing your right foot over the left to start, and for the first 2 lines, take 7 steps and rest on the 8th count.

On the third and fourth lines, reverse the direction. Swing your left leg over your right and walk or skip 8 more steps. Really swing your leg way over—the move is a whole body twist. You get a wonderful feeling when the whole circle does it at the same time.

For the chorus: Your last step was on your right foot. Now, hands on your hips, stamp with your left heel in front of your right foot. At the same time, bring your left shoulder forward and to the right, in a defiant kind of way. Step back, face the circle center and stamp your right heel in front of your left foot. As your right heel comes down, bring your right shoulder forward and twist your body to the left. Really stamp your feet hard. Repeat this step 4 times in all and it will take you through the first two lines of the chorus.

For the last two lines, walk around yourself with small steps, looking over your left shoulder arrogantly. Then join hands and start the dance again with the second stanza.

CHUN-GUM (Chewing Gum)

My mam - ma gave me a pen - ny to buy some can — dy, I
did - n't buy no can - dy, I bought some chun-gum. Chu chu chu chu chu chun-gum, chu
chu chu chun-gum, I did - n't buy no can - dy, I bought some chun-gum.

HOKOPAREPARE

This action song comes from the Maori people in New Zealand. The Maoris had chants for all the ordinary tasks of everyday life, and also for more exciting activities, such as flying a kite! This chant is a children's game and you say just one nonsense word—"hokoparepare"—4 times. Either the leader says it or the whole group can say it as a chorus. Chant it rhythmically like this:

Ho - ko - pa - re - pa - re

As you say the words:

Ho-ko   Slap your thighs (see diagram 1).

Pare-pare   Lift your arms (with elbows bent) out to the side, palms facing forward (see diagram 2).

Ho-ko   Slap your thighs.

Pare-pare   Extend both arms (with straight elbows) diagonally downward to the right side (see diagram 3). Your palms should face towards the back.

Ho-ko   Slap your thighs.

Pare-pare   Same as before, but to the left side (see diagram 4).

Ho-ko   Slap your thighs.

Pare-pare   Lift both elbows to the side, bend your arms in front of you with fingers touching (see diagram 5).

After you memorize the movements, do the entire sequence 6 times through.

Hokoparepare in 4's:

Now the real fun starts, as you use the motions in a "Round" of movement. Since there are 4 separate "hokoparepares," each child gets a number from 1 to 4. If the group is larger, anywhere from 2 to 5 children can use the same number. Before each hokoparepare starts, the leader calls out the next number and signals to the group so it can start the movement sequence on time. Arrange beforehand how many times you want to do the chant so that the groups know when to stop. They will finish one at a time.

Hokoparepare in 8's:

For a more challenging round, give out numbers from 1 to 8. This time, the second group comes in on the "Pare-pare" so that you are breaking the chant down into 8 sections and 8 different starts. Groups 1, 3, 5, and 7 should stand near each other; so should groups 2, 4, 6 and 8. They will be doing the "Ho-ko" movement at the same time, even though their other motions will be different.

If you are feeling very secure, try standing near (or facing) the next numbered group. In this arrangement, each group is always doing a different part of the movement, and it calls for much more concentration. There is a great feeling of satisfaction, though, if you can carry it through to the end.

TARANTELLA

The tarantella, which comes from Italy, is lively and spirited and everyone—from age 6 up—can participate in it and do it well.

The Tarantella Step:

The basic step is easy to learn. Start by stepping out to the right side with your right foot. Then hop on it. Step out with your left foot to the left side and hop on that. After you've gotten the feel of these movements, step and hop on the right, but this time, swing your left foot across the right in front as you hop. Do the same thing (swing your right foot across) when you hop on your left foot. This is the actual tarantella step—a step-hop with a swing over it by the other foot. It is a natural thing to do and it won't give you any trouble.

When you have mastered the basic step, add arm movements. Hold your arms straight up overhead. Bend them a little in the direction of the left foot when you step on it, and a little to the right as you step on your right foot. Snap your fingers in rhythm or clap in rhythm. Even better, if you have a tambourine, shake

it and bang on it—in that order! Keep your body straight and proud. The dance should be done with great dignity and verve.

TARANTELLA (continued)

The Dance

Measures 1 and 2: Form a circle and face the center of it. Do the tarantella step twice—step-hop-right, step-hop-left, step-hop-right, step-hop-left.

Measures 3 and 4: Put one hand on your hip, keep the other hand in the air and pivot in a full turning step to the left (clockwise). Chances are you can make at least 2 complete turns.

Now repeat steps 1 and 2 from the start as Measures 1-4 repeat.

Measures 5 and 6: Bend low, stretch your arms straight behind your back and take 8 small steps to the circle center, gradually lifting your arms and your body. When you reach the center, your arms should be stretched up very high, your body tall—almost leaning back—your head looking up. Shake your hands all through these measures by turning your wrists to simulate the shaking movement of the tambourine. Clap at the end of the 6th measure.

Measures 7 and 8: Re-trace your steps, lowering your arms and your body as you come out of the circle. Clap your hands on the 8th count going out (when you're at the lowest point). Finish the way you started, with your hands behind you, bending low.

Repeat Measures 5-8 and start the dance again from the beginning.

Tarantella with Partners:

Face each other for the first 2 steps. On the turn, put your right arms around each others' waists. Hold your left hands in the air and look at each other as you turn. Younger children can skip, older ones can pivot on the turn.

Tambourines:

If you are lucky enough to have tambourines, you might like to decorate them with strips of crepe paper about 2 feet (65 cm.) long. They will be short enough so that you won't trip on them, but long enough to fly as you move your arms and they give a splendid feeling of motion.

If you don't have tambourines, you can make them. Use 2 paper plates (one inside the other for extra strength) and decorate them with crayon or paint designs. Shellac them—it makes them stronger. Now, with a pencil, punch holes about 2 inches (5 cm.) apart, $\frac{3}{4}$ of the way around the plate, leaving room for your hand to hold the tambourine comfortably. If you can

TARANTELLA

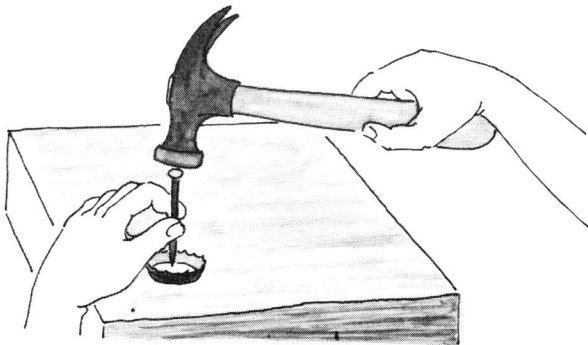

get little bells from a variety store, string them with colored yarn and lace them into the holes. Leave a little bit of yarn around them so they are not strung too tight to shake. If you have enough bells, use 2 for each hole, and your tambourine will have a really good sound. If bells are not available, use bottle tops or caps. Place them on a piece of wood and hammer a nail through them.

String yarn through this hole, just as you would do with the bells, and the caps will shake. You definitely need to put 2 bottle caps into each hole, because the cap needs something to bang against in order to make a sound. Don't forget to add crepe paper streamers— whatever kind of tambourine you use.

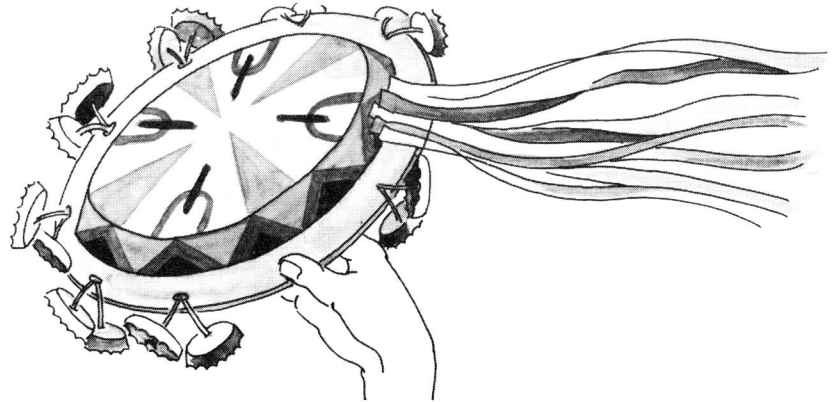

MATATIRU-TIRU-LÁ

Number of players: 10 - 24
(an even number of boys and girls)

Bue - nos dias, su señ - or - í - a. Ma - ta - ti - ru - ti - ru - lá.

This game originated in Spain, but you can find variations of it in South America and Puerto Rico. It is about finding a mate and getting the parents to give their permission.

Choose two children to be Mother and Father. They face each other. Boys join Father's line and girls join Mother's line. All link elbows, with Mother and Father in the center of the rows.

The last boy on the right is the first suitor. As he sings, his entire row skips forward and the girls' line skips backward. As the Mother answers, her line skips forward.

At "De qué oficio la pondría?" the suitor must think of what he wants his wife to do—wash dishes, for example, or go dancing. If this appeals to the Mother ("Ese oficio sí me gusta"), the girl joins the boys' line.

The last girl on the right is the next suitor. She asks the father for a mate from his line. She might want her husband to make beds or change the baby. If the Father is not pleased ("Ese oficio no me gusta!"), the girl must make another suggestion—perhaps going to the movies or playing football. The game continues until everyone has a mate and the lines are totally mixed.

All the conversation is sung. The word "matatiru-tiru-lá" (a nonsense word) follows every line.

Buenos días, su señoría (señorío),
(Good day to you, madam [sir].)
    ¿Qué quería, su señorío (señorita)?
    (What can I do to help you, sir [miss]?)
Yo quería a una (uno) de sus hijas (hijos).
(I want one of your daughters [sons].)
    ¿A cuál de ellas (ellos) le quería?
    (And which one do you want?)
Yo quería a Juanita (Juan)
(or the name of any girl or boy in the line).
(I want Juanita [John].)
    ¿De qué oficio la (lo) pondría?
    (For what job do you want her [him]?)
La (lo) pondría de lavaplatos.
(I want her [him] to wash dishes.)
    Ese oficio sí (no) me gusta.
    (I do [not] like that job.)

When asked what reason you want him or her for, you can make up your own answers. Here are a few:

la (lo) pondría a pagar las cuentas	(pay bills)
la (lo) pondría de bailarina	(go dancing)
la (lo) pondría a hacer las camas	(make beds)
la (lo) pondría de niñera	(change the baby)
la (lo) pondría a hacer las compras	(shop for groceries)
la (lo) pondría a cantarme	(sing for me)

COUNTING RHYMES

Number of players: Unlimited

These classic elimination games are quick contests which decide who is "Out" or select a leader, or "It," for a game. Try them along with the circle games in this book, instead of choosing someone at random to go into the center.

An old English counting rhyme:

> **One, two**
> **Sky blue**
> **All out (in)**
> **But you!**

A South American chant—use it to choose someone to begin a game:

> **La galli<u>na</u> <u>pu</u>so un <u>hue</u>vo.**
> **Puso <u>dos</u>, puso <u>tres</u>, puso <u>cuatro</u>, puso <u>cinco</u>,**
> **Puso <u>seis</u>, puso <u>siete</u>, puso <u>ocho</u>—(pause)**
> **<u>Pan</u> y biz<u>co</u>cho para el <u>burro</u> <u>mo</u>cho**
> **<u>Tuturu</u>tu para que <u>salgas</u> <u>tú</u>.**

> which means

> **The hen <u>laid</u> an <u>egg</u>.**
> **She laid <u>2</u>, laid <u>3</u>, laid <u>4</u>, laid <u>5</u>,**
> **Laid <u>6</u>, laid <u>7</u>, laid <u>8</u>—(pause)**
> **<u>Bread</u> and <u>cake</u> for the <u>short</u>-tailed <u>donkey</u>,**
> **Cock-a-doodle-<u>doo</u>, so you <u>can</u> <u>come</u> <u>out</u>.**

On each underlined or accented word, point to the next person in the circle. Speed up the last 2 lines to double-time. The person you point to at the last word, "tú," is "It" or "Out."

Here are four more count-out rhymes:

> **Wheat germ, yogurt, herbal tea,**
> **Soybeans, carrots, Vitamin C,**
> **My mother eats organically,**
> **So out goes YOU.**

> **Icka backa, icka backa,**
> **Icka backa boo!**
> **Icka backa, soda cracker,**
> **Out goes you!**

> **Charlie Chaplin**
> **Sat on a pin.**
> **How many inches**
> **Did it go in?**
> **Four—(or pick any number)**
> **1-2-3-4. . . .**

Count the number around the circle until you come to the last 4, who is out.

> **Gypsy, gypsy,**
> **Lives in a tent.**
> **Can't afford to pay the rent.**
> **When the rent man comes next day,**
> **Gypsy, gypsy runs away.**
> **And out goes YOU.**

PAT-A-CAKE GAMES

Pat-a-cake is a clapping game done to rhymes with a partner. It is splendid for developing coordination and a sense of rhythm. As you get more skillful, you can design your own clapping patterns, which include clapping hands together in different ways, slapping different parts of your body, and slapping hands with your partner. A good part of the fun, after you have mastered the sequence, is to speed it up and try to hold onto the pattern.

A Sailor Went to Sea, Sea, Sea

Choose partners, face each other and start on the upbeat. On the first line:

A-	Clap your own hands together
sai-	Clap right hands with your partner
-lor	Clap your own hands together
went	Clap left hands with your partner
to	Clap your own hands together
sea, sea, sea	Clap your partner's hands 3 times quickly

Continue this pattern for each line.

For More Challenging Variations:

The next time you sing "sea, sea, sea," jump and turn 3 times in place as you clap. Then try it with 3 jumps in place: on the first jump, cross your feet; on the second jump, land with your feet apart; and on the third, land with your feet together. Don't forget to clap at the same time. The trick here is to remember that after the 3 claps together, the entire series starts again with another clap together—so that actually there are 4 consecutive claps.

PAT-A-CAKE GAMES

El Buenote Sancho Panza

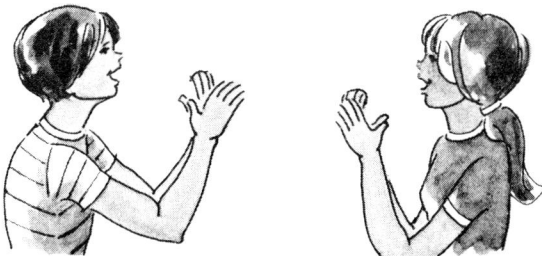

El bue - no - te San - cho Pan - za, za, Ha ma - ta - do a su mu -

- jer jer jer Por-que no ten-ía dí - ne - ro ro. Para írse-para írse-a un ca-fé, fé fé.
(Spoken - accent on "írse")

This pat-a-cake game is about Don Quixote's famous friend, Sancho Panza. Use the same clapping pattern that you used for "A Sailor Went to Sea, Sea, Sea."

El buenote Sancho Panza, za
Ha matado a su mujer jer jer
Porque no tenía dinero ro.
Para írse-para írse-a un café, fé, fé.

which means

The good Sancho Panza, za
Has killed his wife, wife, wife
Because she did not have money
To go-to go-to the café, fé, fé.

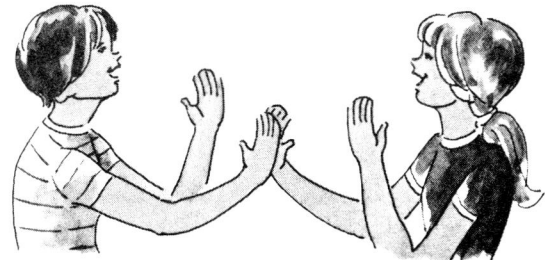

PAT-A-CAKE GAMES

Miss Mary Mack

Spunky

Miss Mar - y Mack — Mack — Mack — All dressed in black — black — black.

Miss Mary Mack, Mack, Mack,
All dressed in black, black, black,
With silver buttons, buttons, buttons,
All down her back, back, back.

She asked her mother, mother, mother,
For fifty cents, cents, cents,
To see the cows, cows, cows,
Jump over the fence, fence, fence.

They jumped so high, high, high,
They reached the sky, sky, sky,
And never came back, back, back,
Till the fourth of July, lie, lie!

This pat-a-cake rhyme doesn't give you a moment's rest.

Here is the pattern for the first line:

Miss	Cross hands and clap your shoulders
Mar-	Uncross arms and clap your thighs
-y	Clap hands together
Mack	Clap right hands with your partner
—(pause)	Clap your own hands together
Mack	Clap left hands with your partner
—(pause)	Clap your own hands together
Mack	Clap both hands across with your partner

Continue the same pattern for the rest of the verses.

Chicken

The pattern goes like this:

C-	Put your hands in prayer position, fingers pointing front, to the right of your body. As you say "C" swing them towards your partner, until both sets of hands meet in a slap
—(pause)	Clap right hands with your partner high
—(pause)	Clap your own hands together
That's the	Clap right hands with your partner low
way it	Clap palms straight ahead with your partner
be-	Clap your own hands together
gins,	Slap backs of both hands with your partner straight ahead
	Clap your own hands together

Continue the same clapping pattern throughout.

PAT-A-CAKE GAMES

Chicken

C — that's the way it be - gins, H — that's the sec - ond let - ter in,

I — I am the third and C — that's the fourth let - ter in that bird, oh

K — I'm fil - lin' in, E — I'm near the N — Oh

C - H - I - C - K - E - N That's the way you spell Chick - en! Oh

Ru - fus Ras - tas John - ston Brown, What-cha gon-na do when the rain comes down?

What-cha gon-na say? What-cha gon-na play? What-cha gon-na do come Judg - ment Day? Oh,

You know I know red means go. Land-lord's gon-na throw us in the snow. Oh,

Ru - fus Ras - tas John - ston Brown, What-cha gon-na do when the rain comes down?

PAT-A-CAKE GAMES

Miss Lucy Had a Baby

Sing this to the tune, "A Sailor Went to Sea, Sea, Sea."

Miss Lucy had a baby.
She named it Tiny Tim.
She put him in the bathtub
To see if he could swim.

He drank up all the water,
He ate up all the soap,
He tried to eat the bathtub
But it wouldn't go down his throat.

Miss Lucy called the Doctor,
Miss Lucy called the Nurse,
Miss Lucy called the lady
With the alligator purse.

Try making up some of your own verses.
Here are some samples:

"Measles," said the Doctor,
"Mumps," said the Nurse,
"A virus," said the lady
With the alligator purse.

"Penicillin," said the Doctor,
"Bed rest," said the Nurse,
"Pizza," said the lady
With the alligator purse.

"He'll live," said the Doctor,
"He's all right," said the Nurse,
"I'm leaving," said the lady
With the alligator purse.

Each syllable has a movement to go with it. Face your partner. Extend bent hands in front of you, chest high, one palm up and one palm down. Your partner's hands should be in the same position, but in reverse.

Here is the clapping pattern:

Miss	Slap your partner's palms once
Lu-	Reverse your hands and slap them again
cy	Clap your own hands together
had	Clap right hands
a	Clap your own hands together
ba-	Clap left hands
by	Clap your own hands together
—(pause)	Clap your own hands together behind your back

Repeat the pattern on each line of the verse. Once you have mastered it, see how fast you can do it without falling apart completely.

BALL-BOUNCING JINGLES

Bouncie Bouncie Ballie

Number of players: Unlimited

Boun - cie, boun - cie, ball - ie. My sis - ter's name is Paul - ie. I gave her a slap, She paid me back, Boun - cie, boun - cie, ball - ie.

Here are some ball-bouncing rhymes to say to yourself (aloud, of course) as you bounce and catch the ball. Starting off with the easy ones:

One Two Three

One, two, three, (turn)
My mother caught a flea, (turn)
She salted it and peppered it (turn on "it")
And gave it to me for tea! (turn)

Pass your leg over the ball on the fourth count, which means on or after the last word of each line.

One Two Three Alary

One, two, three, alary
I spy Mrs. Sairy
Sitting on a dictionary
Just like a green canary.

My Mother Was Born in England

My mother was born in England,
My father was born in France,
And I was born in diapers,
Because I had no pants!

Pass your leg over the ball on the underlined words. To make it harder, do it first with one leg and then with the other, or do one line with one leg and the next line with the other leg.

Sam, Sam, Dirty Old Man

Sam, Sam, dirty old man,
Washed his face in a frying pan,
Combed his hair with the leg of a chair,
And danced with his nose way up in the air!

Pass your leg over the ball on the underlined words.

67

BALL-BOUNCING JINGLES

Little Jumping Joan

(Here am I, lit-tle jump-ing Joan. When no-bo-dy's with me, I'm al-ways a-lone.)

Bounce your ball on this one, and jump at the same time. You may have to bounce the ball a little harder than usual, so you have more time to go up in the air and come down and catch it. Don't forget to sing as you bounce and jump. That means you are doing three things at once, and that's not easy.

Eaper Weeper Chimbley Sweeper

Eaper, weeper, chimbley-<u>sweep</u>er,
<u>Had</u> a wife and couldn't <u>keep</u> her,
<u>Had</u> another, didn't <u>love</u> her,
<u>Up</u> the chimbley he did <u>shove</u> her!

This jingle is the hardest of all rhythmically. Turn your leg over the ball on the first and fourth count (the underlined words).

Fancier bounces:

Catch first with one hand, then with the other, lifting first one leg and then the other over the ball. The most difficult movement is passing your legs over the ball alternately and still catching the ball on time. It is almost like a jump to the side, and you have to start the second leg going as soon as you have lifted the first! Also try clapping between bounces, so your rhythm is bounce-clap-bounce-clap. You have to work fast, because the ball bounces back faster than you think.

Number One

Number one, touch your tongue.
Number two, touch your shoe.
Number three, touch your knee.
Number four, touch the floor.
Number five, learn to jive.
Number six, pick up sticks.
Number seven, go to heaven. (pantomime climbing stairs)
Number eight, shut the gate.
Number nine, touch your spine.
Number ten, do it all again!

This bouncing rhyme combines bouncing, touching, and doing tricks.

Cannibal King with a Big Brass Ring

As you sing this song, bounce your ball in the usual way until you come to the chorus. Then bounce it once each time you say "Dah-di um" and hold it tight, as you smack twice with your lips. On "Dah-di um dum dum dum day," put your arms around yourself and give yourself an enormous hug.

BALL-BOUNCING JINGLES

Cannibal King with a Big Brass Ring

Oh a can-ni-bal king with a big brass ring fell in love with a pret-ty maid, and ev-'ry night in the pale moon light you can hear this ser-en-ade. Dah-di- um smack smack, dah-di - um smack smack, dah-di - um dum dum dum day, dah-di- um smack smack dah-di - um smack smack dah-di - um dum dum dum day.

1

Oh, a cannibal king with a big brass ring
Fell in love with a pretty maid,
And every night in the pale moonlight
You could hear this serenade:

CHORUS

Dah-di um, (smack smack)
Dah-di um (smack, smack)
Dah-di um dum dum dum day.
(and repeat)

2

He would hug and kiss his little miss
Under the bamboo tree,
And every night in the pale moonlight,
It would sound like this to me:

69

JUMP ROPE GAMES

Take out a good length of clothesline, round up your friends (at least 5 of them) and jump rope!

All in Together

If a large group is playing (more than 10), use two ropes. With 2 turners for each rope, it won't be too crowded and you'll have more chance to jump, instead of waiting so long for a turn. Everyone starts in the rope:

> All in together, girls (boys or kids)
> How do you like the weather, girls? (boys, kids)
> January, February, March, April—

Each child jumps out of the rope on the month of his or her birthday, so by the time the chant is over, everyone is out. Reverse it by saying the chant again. This time each child jumps in when the birthday month is called.

Every Morning

Many jump rope jingles end with numbers. Then the children holding the ends of the rope turn it very fast, trying to get the jumper out. The numbers become a countdown.

> Every morning at 8 o'clock,
> You can hear the postman knock.
> Up jumps Mary (John) to open the door—
> 1 letter, 2 letters, 3 letters, 4, 5, 6 . . .

> Every night at half-past ten,
> Mary (Johnny) takes a bath again,
> She (he) scrubs her back and soaps her skin—
> How many minutes is Mary (Johnny) in? 1, 2 . . .

> Every evening at half-past six,
> Out come the trousers for Mary (Johnny) to fix,
> How many patches did she (he) sew on? 1, 2, 3 . . .

> Every day at ten of three,
> Mary (Johnny) pets her bumble bee,
> She pets him high and she pets him low,
> How many times did he sting her toe? 1, 2, 3 . . .

> Every noon at twelve o'clock,
> Mary (Johnny) makes the cradle rock.
> She rocks it fast without a doubt,
> How many times till the baby falls out? 1, 2, 3 . . .

Mabel, Mabel

> Mabel, Mabel, strong and able,
> Keep your elbows off the table.
> This is not a horses' stable
> But a first class dining table!
> SALT, MUSTARD, VINEGAR, PEPPER!

On the word "Pepper," the rope-turners speed up and turn as fast as they can.

House for Rent

> House for rent,
> Inquire within.
> When I move out,
> Let Jimmy move in!

Jimmy then jumps in and the game continues, until he calls someone else to move in, and the jumping goes on until everyone has had a turn.

JUMP ROPE GAMES

Down the Mississippi

Two people jump at the same time in the next jingles, one behind the other. The second child pushes the first, who jumps out. As the chant begins again, the next child jumps in, and pushes out the second. The game continues until everyone has had a chance to jump in, push, and be pushed.

Down the Mississippi where the boats go push—!

No mistake, there is really only one line to this jingle!

Mother Got

Mother got the whooping cough,
Father got the gout,
Sister got the chicken pox,
And brother pushed her OUT!

You can do these alone or with your friends:

Sneeze

Sneeze on Monday, sneeze for danger.
Sneeze on Tuesday, kiss a stranger.
Sneeze on Wednesday, get a letter,
Sneeze on Thursday, something better.
Sneeze on Friday, sneeze for sorrow,
Sneeze on Saturday, fun tomorrow!

Spanish Jump Rope

Un cocherito, leré	A baby carriage, leré
Me dijo un día, leré	Asked me one day, leré
Que si queria, leré	If I would like to, leré
Pasear en coche, leré.	Travel by carriage, leré.
Y yo le dijo, leré	And I responded, leré
Con gransalero, leré	With great dignity, leré
Que me mareo, leré	That I got dizzy, leré.

El nombre de María	The name of Maria
Que cinco letras tiene,	Which has five letters,
Que la M (pronounced emmay)	With an M
Que la A (pronounced ah)	With an A
Que la R (pronounced erray)	With an R
Que la Í (pronounced eee)	With an I
Que la A (pronounced ah)	With an A
MA-RÍ-A!	MA-RI-A!

In the last stanza, use the jumper's name. When you shout it out on the last line, the rope-turners speed up and turn as fast as they can to make you miss.

Cinderella

Cinderella, dressed in yella,
Went upstairs to kiss a fella,
Made a mistake and kissed a snake,
And came downstairs with a belly ache.

I Was in the Garden

I was in the garden
A-picking of the peas—
I busted out a-laughing
To hear the cabbage sneeze!

INDEX AND AGE RANGES